THE MIRACLES OF MARY

A Seventeenth–Century Ethiopian Manuscript

Kathleen Bickford Berzock

THE ART INSTITUTE OF CHICAGO

This publication has been generously
supported by donations from
The African American Gala Fund,
Mary Carol Fee, George Mann,
Terry and Cynthia Perucca, and The
Woman's Board in honor of docent
Martha McCallister's 30th anniversary.

*The Miracles of Mary: A Seventeenth-Century
Ethiopian Manuscript* appears in
conjunction with the exhibition
organized by The Art Institute of
Chicago and presented from
October 5, 2002, to May 18, 2003.

First edition
Printed in the U.S.A.

Published by
The Art Institute of Chicago
111 South Michigan Avenue
Chicago, Illinois 60603-6110

ISBN 0-86559-200-4
Library of Congress Control
Number: 2002112235

Produced by the Publications
Department of The Art Institute of
Chicago, Susan F. Rossen,
Executive Director
Edited by Britt Salvesen
Production by Sarah E. Guernsey
Designed by Jeff Wonderland
Photography and separations by
the Imaging Department,
Alan B. Newman, Executive Director
Map by Mapping Specialists,
Madison, Wis.
Printed by Chicago Press Corporation

Front cover:
Detail of plate 7
Page 6:
Detail of plate 10
Back cover:
Detail of plate 1

Acknowledgments

This publication is the result of the dedicated efforts of many people. However, it would have remained only a dream without the generous financial contributions of The African American Gala Fund, Mary Carol Fee, George Mann, Terry and Cynthia Perucca, and The Woman's Board in honor of docent Martha McCallister's 30th anniversary. Thus, my thanks are extended to them first and foremost.

I am equally grateful for the assistance of the many scholars of Ethiopian art, history, and culture who have willingly and patiently allowed me, a non-specialist, to consult with them. My sincere thanks go to Dr. David Appleyard, School of Oriental and African Studies, University of London; Dr. Donald Crummey, University of Illinois at Urbana-Champaign; Dr. Gene Gragg, University of Chicago; Dr. Getatchew Haile, Hill Monastic Manuscript Library, St. John's University; Dr. Marilyn E. Heldman, University of Missouri– St. Louis; Dr. Donald Levine, University of Chicago; and Dr. Ray Silverman, University of Michigan. Any errors contained in the text are my own.

Within the museum, I appreciate the support and encouragement of James N. Wood, Director and President, and Richard F. Townsend, Curator in the Department of African and Amerindian Art. The talented staffs of many Art Institute departments have worked together to make this project a success. For their outstanding work on the publication, my warmest thanks are due to Susan F. Rossen, Sarah Guernsey, and Britt Salvesen in the Publications Department; Alan Newman, Chris Gallagher, Eva Panek, and Greg Williams in the Imaging Department; Lyn DelliQuadri and Jeff Wonderland in the Department of Graphic Design and Communication Services; and Brent Riley in the Museum Shop. I am also grateful to Margo McFarland in the Department of Prints and Drawings; Hannah Bennett, Barbara Korbel, Lauren Lessing, and Susan Perry in the Ryerson and Burnham Libraries; Jane Clarke, Clare Kunny, Maria Marable-Bunch, and Rita McCarthy in the Department of Museum Education; Linda Steele, Director of Community Relations; and Ray Ramirez, Barbara Battaglia, and Leah Bowe in the Department of African and Amerindian Art. Finally, I offer special thanks to Jane Clarke, Lyn DelliQuadri, Sarah Guernsey, and Brent Riley for their encouragement and enthusiasm from beginning to end.

Kathleen Bickford Berzock
Associate Curator for African Art

SINCE ITS EARLIEST FOUNDATIONS IN THE fourth century, Ethiopian Orthodox Christianity has developed a unique character and distinctive forms of practice. Notably, the figure of Mary is invested with wide-ranging and deeply resonant meanings in Ethiopia, where she is honored as the Holy Mother of God, the Mother Church, and Our Lady Mary the Intercessor, who prevails upon her Son to forgive the sins of humanity.

Texts describing miracles performed by Mary, such as the healing of infirmities or forgiveness of sins, first became popular in France in the twelfth century and arrived in Ethiopia via Spain, Palestine, and Egypt. These Latin texts were translated into Arabic and then into Ge'ez, the ancient and liturgical language of Christian Ethiopia, in the fourteenth century. Mary's significance in Ethiopia intensified in the mid-fifteenth century, during the reign of Emperor Ze'ra Ya'equob (r. 1434–68).[2]

Ze'ra Ya'equob decreed the integration of readings about Mary into daily Church ritual; the establishment of more than thirty feast days in commemoration of her; and the compilation and translation of Marian writings, including the recording of her miracles. In Ethiopian accounts, the number of miracles credited to Mary expanded to over three hundred, and after Ze'ra Ya'equob's initiatives the Miracles of Mary became one of the most popular themes for religious books, which served to guide worshipers through the yearly cycle of celebrations for the Virgin.

In the mid-1600s, following a century of warfare with neighboring Muslims and other factions that included the destruction of churches and religious art, Christian Ethiopia experienced a period of renewal. A permanent capital was established at Gonder, in northwest Ethiopia (see map, p.9), and the city soon became a center of artistic innovation. There, artists working for the glory of the Church painted murals and devotional images, made processional crosses of metal and wood, and produced richly illustrated manuscripts. The arts of calligraphy and manuscript illumination in particular were among the most prominent and sophisticated of the era; at scriptoria staffed by lay clergy in Gonder, and probably also in nearby Azazo, royal patrons could commission luxurious manuscripts for themselves and for presentation to monasteries and churches.[3] Artists and craftsmen engaged in religious work achieved a higher social status than their counterparts who labored making secular objects, but they were nevertheless expected to maintain a proper humility, and today their names are mostly unknown.[4]

The lavish *Miracles of Mary* now in the collection of The Art Institute of Chicago dates from the mid-to-late seventeenth century, and bears the effects of many years of careful use. The manuscript comprises 158 pages, and includes 71 paintings, which are protected by cotton veils that are tied directly to the tops of the pages. The book is bound between wooden boards that are covered with finely tooled morocco leather. These boards are original, but the spine has been replaced and the book rebound, probably in the twentieth century.

The Art Institute's *Miracles of Mary* is one of a group of closely related manuscripts believed to have been produced at a single scriptorium in Gonder.[5] Although all are thought to be based on a common archetype, these versions are not mere duplicates; each shows a personal approach to illustration that bespeaks the creativity of artists working in proximity and inspired by one another. Here, the uniformity of the script suggests that the volume is the work of a single gifted calligrapher. Likewise, the paintings exhibit a stylistic

MAP OF PRESENT-DAY ETHIOPIA

consistency that could only be produced by an individual artist.

The illustrations in the Art Institute's manuscript are excellent examples of the style known to scholars as the First Gonderine, after the capital city. This manner of painting is distinguished by the bold outlines used for the figures, schematic shading that enlivens the faces, linear rendering of drapery and hair, an emphasis on decorative textile patterns, and often whimsical depictions of architecture. Artists employed a rich but restricted palette of red, yellow, blue, and green, setting forms against flat, unelaborated backgrounds. While the figures' faces show little expression, their gestures and interactions convey freshness and vitality. In addition, Gonderine-style compositions tend to present narratives of varying complexity, featuring identifiable religious personages and making reference to the dress and furnishings of the day. The narratives are reinforced by captions—probably added by the calligrapher— that identify people and objects in the scenes. The depiction of different races and ethnicities is worth remarking upon, as it too is based on contemporary experience. Although they repre- sent characters from religious texts, most of the figures in the Art Institute's *Miracles of Mary* are portrayed in the guise of Christian Ethiopians, with dark hair, oval faces, and long noses; by contrast, aggressors have large bodies and bulbous heads, and wear turbans and wide-legged short pants (see plate 2). These figures are probably Muslims, reflecting periodic conflicts between the Christians of Ethiopia and their Islamic neighbors.

The text is written on parchment—the specially prepared, fine-grained skin of a cow, sheep, or goat—in three columns of fifteen lines each, using an elegant script called *gweleh* that is distinctive for its clarity and regularity (see plate 10). The calligrapher relied upon scored lines, still visible on the manuscript's pages, to align the text precisely. The illuminator used sheets of the same scored parchment, indicating that the volume was conceived as a unified whole, incorporating words and images. Unlike the calligrapher, however, the illuminator purpose-

fully disregarded the structure of the columns. This compositional freedom, together with the fact that such manuscript paintings exhibit many stylistic affinities with religious murals of the time, suggests that manuscript painters were not trained exclusively as illuminators.[6]

As in other Gonderine collections treating this theme, the text is principally devoted to the standard canon of thirty-two Marian miracles, each illustrated with a narrative painting (see plates 5–11).[7] These are preceded by prayers, hymns, and three illustrated stories from the Life of the Virgin (plates 1–4), and are followed by depictions of the Passion of Christ, Christ in Judgment (plate 12), saints, and martyrdom. As is common in manuscripts from this period, the name of the man who commissioned the book, Walada Iyasus, along with the names of his parents, were originally written into the text. References to Walada Iyasus and his family were later erased and replaced in all but one location by the names of a subsequent owner, Kirubel; his wife, Kola Gannat; and in some sections his parents (see plate 10, top of third column of text). Owners also recorded important transactions in such books; here, two notes concerning the sale of land are appended to the text, one at the front and one at the back. These annotations appear in Amharic, the language spoken by most Christian Ethiopians.

This spectacular manuscript speaks to the longevity and unique character of Christianity in Ethiopia, in particular the reverence offered to Mary, the Holy Mother of God. Through the arts such devotion was nurtured and enhanced. The intimate contemplation that this book inspires is a testament to the skill of the artists who made it and to the compelling nature of the stories it contains.

1. Marilyn E. Heldman, "Maryam Seyon: Mary of Zion," in Roderick Grierson, ed., *African Zion: The Sacred Art of Ethiopia* (New Haven: Yale University Press, 1993), pp. 71–72; Getatchew Haile, "Daily Life and Religious Practice in Ethiopia," in Baltimore, The Walters Art Museum, *Ethiopian Art: The Walters Art Museum* (Lingfield, U.K.: Third Millennium Publishing, 2001), p. 36.

2. Getatchew Haile, "The Mariology of Emperor Zär'a Ya'eqob of Ethiopia," *Orientalia Christiana Analecta*, 242 (Rome: Pontificium Institutum Studiorum Orientalium, 1992), pp. 1–2; Marilyn E. Heldman, *The Marian Icons of the Painter Frē Seyon: A Study in Fifteenth-Century Ethiopian Art, Patronage, and Spirituality* (Wiesbaden: Harrassowitz, 1994), pp. 165–68.

3. Ibid.; and Heldman in Grierson 1993 (note 1), p. 194.

4. Marilyn E. Heldman, "Creating Religious Art: The Status of Artisans in Highland Christian Ethiopia," *Aethiopica: International Journal of Ethiopian Studies* 1 (1998), p. 132.

5. Ibid., p. 195; see Guy Annequin, "L'Illustration des Ta'amra Maryam de 1630 à 1730: Quelques remarques sur le premier style de Gondar," *Annales d'Éthiopie* 9 (1972), pp. 196–99, for a partial list of collections containing similar manuscripts.

6. Griffith C. Mann, "The Role of the Illuminated Manuscript in Ethiopian Culture," in Baltimore 2001 (note 1), pp. 95, 108.

7. The description of the contents of the manuscript is based on David Appleyard's summary translation, "Miracles of Mary, together with Various Hymns (Salam) and Prayers for Intercession, and Three Stories from the Life of the Virgin Mary," photocopy in the Department of African and Amerindian Art, Art Institute of Chicago, n.d.; Marilyn Heldman refers to this group of miracles as the "standard Gonderine courtly scriptorium collection" and notes that only in Gonderine-style manuscripts are they consistently given narrative illustrations (personal communication, July 9, 2002).

የሁሉ፡ምስለ፡ገብ

ራ፡ኪ፡ኂቤ፡ሕ፡ወ፡ዖስ
ሰ፡ዖስ፡ሰ፡ብእ፡ሲ፡ተ፡ኮጽ፡ገነተ፡

ዘነመ፡ነገሮሙ፡መልአክ፡እንዘ፡ይብል፡
ትወልዱ፡ወለተ፡ጸ፡ሎት፡ከሙ፡በጸሐ፡
ቅድ፡መ፡እግዚ፡አብሔ፡ርጀ

ለዓለም፡ዓለም

ዘነመ፡ተከዙ፡
ኤያቄም፡ወሐና፡

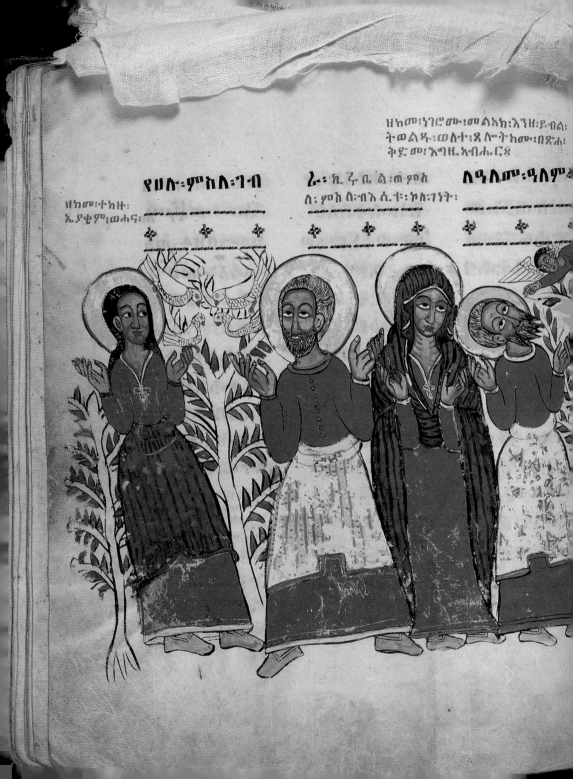

ዘአመ፡ ሐሩ፡ውስተ፡መቅደ፡ ኢ፡የቴም፡ወሐና፡ለ

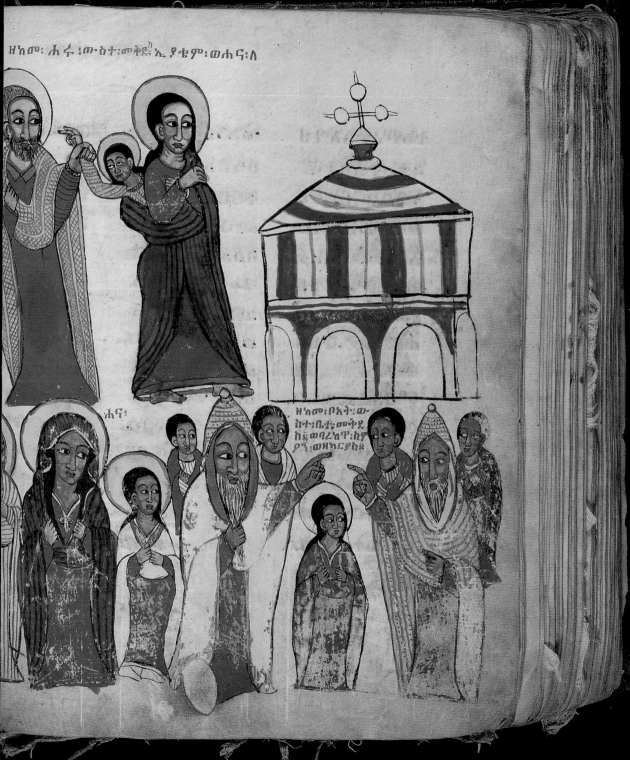

ሐና፡

ዘአመ፡ቦአተ፡ው
ስተ፡ቤተ፡መቅደ
ስ፡ወገብረ፡ከዋ፡ስ
ያን፡ወዘዘአርስ

ዘከመ፡ዒ ስየተ፡ማርያም፡
እግዝእትነ፡ማርያም፡በሳልሳተ፡

ሰዓታ

ዘመ፡ተ ነገሩ
እነ፡ለማርያም፡

ወቃብ ተ፡
ወቃብር፡

ወል

ኪሩ
ቤ፡

ኪ ናት፡

ወልታ

Plate 2

Plate 5

ሠዕለ፡እግዝእት፡
ነ፡ማርያም፡ወፉ
ቀረ፡ወልዳ፡

ዘአመ፡ሰስለ፡ነቤ
ሃ፡ዘእብን፡ጌግሩ፡

ተፈ፡ወ
ሲ፡ዘእ
ግሩ፡

እ፡በን፡ዘወድቀት፡
እምእግሩ፡

ዘአመ፡ቀልአ፡አልባሲ
ሁ፡ዘእብን፡እግፉ፡ወአ
ዕሉሰለ፡ቀ፡ዳዳት፡አመ፡
ኮ፡ኮነ፡ሐያወ፡

110

ዓለም፡አሜን፨   ምነ፡ሕማም፡ዘ   ሠጺቀ፨ከመ፡ዘየ

_____   ታረምጸ፨ማርያ   ሬኢ፡በመጸሐት

ለመርቆሬዎ፡ከ   ም፡ምልኢ፡ለሕሲ   ገጸ፨

ከን፡ዘ አንጻሕኪ፡   ናየ፡ሕፀዖቀሰወል

ለምጸ፨ወ አሕየ   ድኪ፡መምሕረ፡ሕ   ✦✦✦

ወኪዩ፡ፉጸ፡መ፡ አ   ግ፡ኢይርሳዕ፡ተግ

Plate 8

ዘከመ፡እርእዮ
መርቆሬዎክ፡አረ
ዶ፡ኡ፡ከመ፡ሐዪወ
እምለምዴ፡

ዘከመ፡እርእዮ፡መርቆሬዎ
ቅ፡ለእ፡ካርያስ፡ዘዘይደ፡ሥ
ጋሁ፡

ዘከመ፡ቀደስ፡መርቆ
ሬ፡ዎክ፡ድሳረ፡ሐየወ
እምለምዴ፡

ዘከመ፡ተረፈ፡ዐሥ
ለእግዚአትኔ፡ግራ
ያምር፡በውሂበዚሁ፡
ሳብስት፡ወብኡ፡
ሜኪ

ቤተ፡ባሮክ

ዘከመ፡ተመጠ፡ወይን፡
ለእኒ፡ለባሮክ

ማዕድ፡ወፋ
ግለት

እለ፡ይመስሑ፡ሉብኒ፡በቤተ፡ባሮክ

እሱኒ፡ቀሉፋት

Plate 9

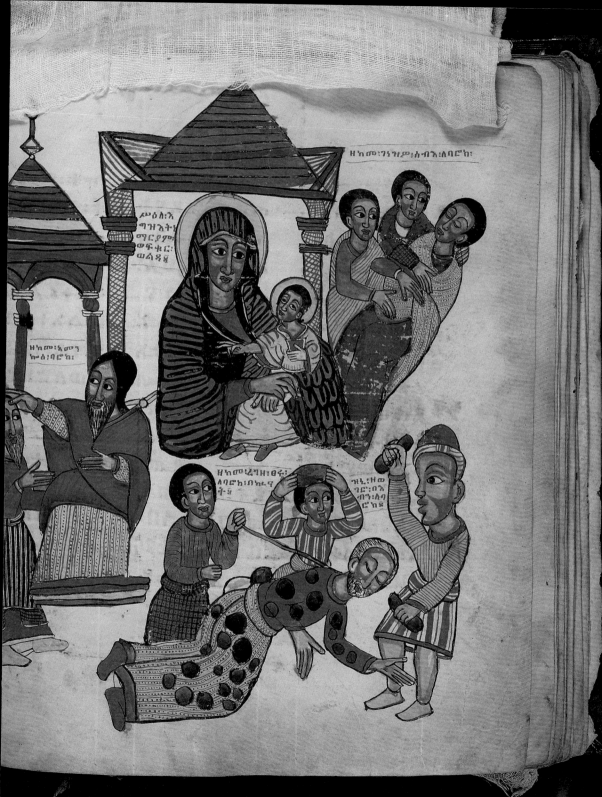

ከማሁ፡ትሬክብ፡	ወተንሥኡ፡እም	ሁሉ፡ምክለ
ፍሥሐ፡ወእም	ክክቡ፡በዐቢይ፡	ራ፡ኪሩቤ ሳ
ይእዜስ፡ትሄሉ፡	ፍሥሐ፠ወበጊዜ	ለዓለመ፡ዓለ
ምክሌዩ፡ውክተ፡	ተንሥኡ፡ወፅ	ታቦተ፡አምላ
ትፍሥሕት፡ዘለ	እት፡ነፍሱ፡እም	ማርያም ትት
ዓለም፡፡ወሰብ፡ሰ	ሥጋሁ፠ወዓርገ	ኒ፡ውቱሪ፠ወ
ምዓ፡ውእቱ፡ዲ	ት፡ምክለ፡እግዝ	ቅድስና፡ጹራ
ያቆን፡ዘንተ፡ነገሪ	እትነ፡ቅድስት፡	ወእክ፡ብሩ
እምአፉሁ፡ለእግ	ማርያም ወለዲ	አንክጣከየ
ዝእትነ፡ቅድስቲ	ተ፡አምላክ፠ወበ	ብርኪ፡አመ
ድንግል፡ማርያ	አት፡ውክት፡ትፍ	ዌሁ፡ተጽዕ
ም፡ወለዲተ፡አም	ሥሕት፡ዘለዓለ	ክመ፡አብስ
ላክ፡ረክበ፡ናህዩ	ም፠ጸሎታ፡ወበ	የ፡ዘያክተራ
ወመሰሎ፡ዘሐይ	ረክታ፡ወምሕረቲ	ሕ፡ነገራ፠ብስ
ወ፡እምደዌሁ፠	ፍቁር፡ወልዴ፡የ	ስላም፡አስም

ጋይ፨እንበሉ፡ሕ   ሰማይ፨ምንትኑ፡   ያም፡በሕርይ

ፍነ፡ማይ፡ዘቆመ፡   ለእንሉ፡እመሕየ   ───────

በገቡ፡ነዳይ፨ክን   ው፡ሠናይ፨እንበ   ፨   ፨

ቱ፡ክንቱ፡በታሕቱ፡   ለፍቅር ኪ፡ማር

Plate II

ሞዓ፡ከ፡ፈሲ፡አዴከ፡

Plate 12

መላእክት፡

ወእሙ፡ይመጽእ፡ወልደ፡እን፡ለ፡እመሕየው፡

ኃጥአን፡

ዳድቃን፡

ኃይ፡በኵሉ፡

The Miracles of Mary (Te'amire Maryam)
Late 17th century, reign of Yohannes (1667–82) or Iyyasu I (1682–1706)
Gonder, Ethiopia
Bound manuscript: Parchment, ink, tempera, wood, leather, cotton, and string
Ada Turnbull Hertle and Marian and Samuel Klasstorner Endowments, 2002.4

INTERPRETATIONS OF THE ILLUSTRATIONS were informed by David Appleyard's summary translation of the Art Institute's manuscript, "Miracles of Mary, together with Various Hymns (Salam) and Prayers for Intercession, and Three Stories from the Life of the Virgin Mary" (photocopy in the Department of African and Amerindian Art, The Art Institute of Chicago, n.d.), and by E. A. Wallis Budge's *Legends of Our Lady Mary the Perpetual Virgin and Her Mother Hanna* (London, 1933) and *One Hundred and Ten Miracles of Our Lady Mary* (London, 1933). The numbers in smaller type indicate the location of the images in the manuscript.

Plate 1
THE STORY OF ANNA AND JOACHIM
When Anna and Joachim were unable to conceive
a child, God took pity on them. On the left,
God comes to them in the form of white birds
above their heads. Next, an angel tells them
they will have a daughter. On the right, Anna
and Joachim take the infant Mary, who will
utimately become Christ's mother, to the Temple.
Below, she receives the blessings, of the elders,
Simeon and Zacharias. The illustration's protective
cotton veil is clearly visible, folded at the top
of the left-hand page.

(28 verso/29 recto)

Plate 2
THE STORY OF MARY AT GOLGOTHA
After Christ's death, Mary went regularly to
Golgotha to pray at his tomb. In an Ethiopian
telling of this story, when the tomb guards harassed
her, Christ made her invisible to them. On the
left-hand page, Mary stands in prayer while the
unwitting guards sit on the ground near Christ's
schematically rendered tomb, surrounded by
their shields and spears. Next, the risen Christ
addresses his Mother. The right-hand page shows
prophets and angels worshiping the Virgin.

(46 verso/47 recto)

Plate 3
CHRIST AND MARY ENTHRONED
Ethiopian tradition holds that after Christ's death,
angels lifted Mary to heaven, where her Son
comforted her and showed her his kingdom.
Here, angels and the righteous surround Christ
and Mary, seated together on a fabric-covered
throne. The prophets appear below them, and
King David sits on the right, playing a *begena*,
a type of Ethiopian harp.

(48 recto)

Plate 4
THE COVENANT OF MERCY
The Covenant of Mercy celebrates Christ's
promise to accept Mary's intercessions on behalf
of humanity—a promise that is honored each time
Mary performs a miracle of salvation or healing.
Here, Jesus gives his covenant to Mary amid
surrounding angels. In Ethiopia the Feast of the
Covenant of Mercy, *Kidane Mehret*, is celebrated
yearly on February 23.

(51 recto)

Plate 5
MIRACLE 1, THE STORY OF
SAINT ILDEPHONSUS OF TOLEDO

Saint Ildephonsus of Toledo (d. 667) is said to
be the original author of the *Miracles of Mary*, which
he wrote to demonstrate his great love for her.
To honor him for his devotion, Mary appeared
before him, blessed him, and presented him with
gifts. On the left, Ildephonsus, with pen in hand,
presents his book to the Virgin. On the right,
Mary gives Ildephonsus a divine robe and throne.
Below, the Archangel Gabriel spears a bishop
who has tried to sit on Ildephonsus's throne after
his death. This story celebrates a founder of
Marian writing and promises divine blessing to
all who describe or illustrate Mary's miracles.

(59 verso/60 recto)

Plate 6
MIRACLE 21, THE STORY OF
THE DYER OF NAZIB

The theme of conflict between Christians and
Muslims was particularly relevant to seventeenth-
century Ethiopians, who had survived a century of
violent warfare between these and other competing
factions. In this story, Nazib, a Christian and a
textile dyer by trade, tries to prevent a Muslim from
stealing a robe. The Muslim then falsely accuses
Nazib, and the dyer is sent to prison. On the right,
Saint George—at Mary's request—orders Nazib's
release; below, priests read Nazib's letter of pardon.

(106 verso/107 recto)

Plate 7
MIRACLE 22, THE STORY OF
THE CLUBFOOTED MAN

The *Miracles of Mary* have their roots in medieval
times, when illness and infirmity were sometimes
perceived as God's punishment for sinfulness,
and the curing of such conditions constituted a
form of redemption. These beliefs obviously
resonated with Ethiopians. In this story, a man
shows his clubfoot to an archbishop in the pres-
ence of a congregation. Next, the man prays
to Mary—who holds a diminutive Christ Child in
her arms—and is cured. The man then displays
his healed foot to the archbishop.

(109 verso/110 recto)

Plate 8
MIRACLE 23, THE STORY OF
THE LEPER BISHOP MERCURIUS

Bishop Mercurius, a victim of leprosy, was
ordered to leave the priesthood because his body
had become impure. Here, Mercurius shows his
disease-ridden body to the archbishop. He then
prays to Mary and is healed. On the right,
Bishop Mercurius reveals to an acolyte and to the
archbishop that he has been cured. Finally, he is
reinstated to the priesthood and celebrates Mass.

(111 verso/112 recto)

Plate 9
MIRACLE 26, THE STORY OF BAROK OF FINQE

Though dissolute, Barok of Finqe loved the Virgin and regularly honored her by hosting a banquet for the poor and needy on the festival of her death. On the left, Barok serves a distinctly Ethiopian feast to his guests, with a communal plate and shapely ceramic jugs. On the right, Mary presides over Barok's ordination as a monk, his death by stoning at the hands of his enemies, and his burial in a state of grace.

(120 verso/121 recto)

Plate 10
MIRACLE 27, THE STORY OF THE DEACON ANASTASIUS

The Deacon Anastasius of Constantinople (now Istanbul) led a life of devotion to the Virgin; here, he prays to her. Then, on his deathbed, Mary appears to him and offers him comfort. The facing page is covered with the stately *gweleh* script used throughout the manuscript. In the first and second columns, Mary's name appears in red ink, while in the third column the name of the original owner has been erased and replaced by the names of a subsequent owner, Kirubel, and his parents. The decorative punctuation used throughout indicates transitions between phrases.

(122 verso/123 recto)

Plate 11
MIRACLE 29, THE STORY OF THE CANNIBAL OF QEMER

In her role as intercessor between Christ and humanity, Mary may plead for even the most depraved sinner if he has once shown repentance. The story of the cannibal of Qemer is perhaps the ultimate example of Mary's compassion. On the left, the cannibal sits before a group of decapitated corpses in the act of eating his wife. Next, the cannibal offers a drink of water to a beggar while a farmer and his family flee from him. On the right, Christ orders demons to take the cannibal's soul—portrayed as a miniature figure—to hell. Mary then intercedes, literally pulling the cannibal's soul up by the hand. Below, angels weigh the water that the cannibal gave to the beggar against the lives of his seventy-eight victims.

(130 verso/131 recto)

Plate 12
SAINT BASILEDES; CHRIST IN JUDGMENT

On the left, Saint Basiledes—one of the many soldier saints, including Saint George (see plate 6), who have been popular in Ethiopia for centuries—rides a white stallion adorned with fine trappings. On the right, a serene and monumental Christ, clothed in richly detailed robes, sits in judgment. With his right hand, Christ invites the blessed to rise up to the angels in heaven, while with his left he gestures for the damned to be dragged by demons into the fires of hell.

(151 verso/152 recto)

SOURCES CONSULTED

Annequin, Guy. "L'Illustration des Ta'amra Maryam de 1630 à 1730: Quelques remarques sur le premier style de Gondar." *Annales d'Éthiopie* 9 (1972), pp. 193–226.

Appleyard, David. *Ethiopian Manuscripts*. London: Jed Press, 1993.

Baltimore, The Walters Art Museum. *Ethiopian Art: The Walters Art Museum*. Lingfield, U.K.: Third Millennium Publishing, 2001.

Budge, E. A. Wallis. *Legends of Our Lady Mary the Perpetual Virgin and Her Mother Hanna*. London: Oxford University Press, 1933.

———. *One Hundred and Ten Miracles of Our Lady Mary*. London: Oxford University Press, 1933.

Chojnacki, Stanislaw, in collaboration with Carolyn Gossage. *Ethiopian Icons: Catalogue of the Collection of the Institute of Ethiopian Studies, Addis Ababa University*. Milan: Skira, 2000.

Getatchew Haile. "Builders of Churches and Authors of Hymns: Makers of History in the Ethiopian Church." In *Études éthiopiennes: Actes de la Xe conférence internationale des études éthiopiennes*, vol. I. Paris: Société française pour les études éthiopiennes, 1994.

———. "The Mariology of Emperor Zär'a Ya'eqob of Ethiopia." *Orientalia Christiana Analecta*, 242. Rome: Pontificium Institutum Studiorum Orientalium, 1992.

Grierson, Roderick, ed. *African Zion: The Sacred Art of Ethiopia*. New Haven: Yale University Press, 1993.

Heldman, Marilyn E. "Creating Religious Art: The Status of Artisans in Highland Christian Ethiopia." *Aethiopica: International Journal of Ethiopian Studies* I (1998), pp. 131–47.

———. "Frē Seyon: A Fifteenth-Century Ethiopian Artist." *African Arts* 31, 4 (1998), pp. 48–55, 90.

———. *The Marian Icons of the Painter Frē Seyon: A Study in Fifteenth-Century Ethiopian Art, Patronage, and Spirituality*. Wiesbaden: Harrassowitz, 1994.

LeRoy, Jules. *Ethiopian Painting in the Late Middle Ages and during the Gondar Dynasty*. New York: Frederick A. Praeger, 1964.

Mercier, Jacques. *Art that Heals: The Image as Medicine in Ethiopia*. New York: Prestel/The Museum for African Art, 1997.

Silverman, Ray, ed. *Ethiopia: Traditions of Creativity*. East Lansing/Seattle: Michigan State University Museum in association with the University of Washington Press, 1999.